GB

MIDLOTHIAN LIBRARY SERVICE

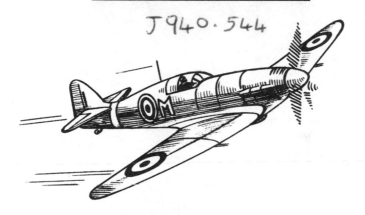

WORLD WAR II STORIES
WAR IN THE
AIR

J 940.544

ANTHONY MASTERS

Illustrated by Joyce Macdonald

W
FRANKLIN WATTS
LONDON•SYDNEY

Editor Belinda Hollyer
Editor-in-Chief John C. Miles
Design Billin Design Solutions
Art Director Jonathan Hair

First published in 2004
by Franklin Watts
96 Leonard Street
London
EC2A 4XD

Franklin Watts Australia
45-51 Huntley Street
Alexandria
NSW 2015

ISBN 0 7496 4804 X

A CIP catalogue record for this book is available
from the British Library.

Printed in Great Britain

CONTENTS

PROLOGUE

Control of the air was essential in the Second World War. Everyone knew that however well the army and navy were doing, they had to be backed by an effective air force. Without air support, an army and navy were always in danger.

The British and German air forces fought each other in the Battle of Britain. The pilots and crews on both sides were brave and resourceful. The success of the Royal Air Force (the RAF) saved Britain from being invaded by Germany, and meant that the British could keep fighting against Hitler.

The second story is about another kind of courage. Franz Von Werra, a Luftwaffe (German air force) pilot, managed to escape from captivity – not just once, but many times. War stories often celebrate individuals like him, who had extraordinary courage and determination. Such people were secret weapons for their country.

In the war with Japan, American forces in the Pacific fought Japanese pilots who used their aeroplanes as direct weapons. Instead of dropping bombs, the planes themselves were the bombs, flown straight into Allied targets. The Japanese suicide pilots – like suicide bombers in modern times – were prepared to die, in order to destroy those they believed were enemies.

The Japanese continued to fight in the Pacific after Germany had surrendered. Th Allied forces were desperate to bri war to a final end. They d new and terrible

On 6 August 1945, an atomic bomb was dropped on the Japanese city of Hiroshima. On 9 August 1945 a second atomic bomb was dropped on the city of Nagasaki. Japan surrendered the next day.

Thousands of people were killed or injured by the atomic bombs. Still more people suffered long term radiation effects from the two explosions.

THE BATTLE OF
BRITAIN

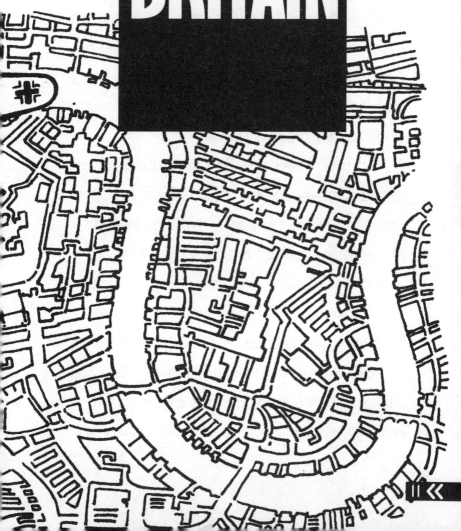

Britain and France declared war on Germany on 3 September 1939. But by the following June, France had been defeated. The British Expeditionary Force, which had been sent to support the French army, retreated to Dunkirk. The soldiers were brought home to Britain by hundreds of small British boats which sailed across the channel to rescue them.

By June 1940, the British expected an immediate invasion by Germany. But the days and weeks passed, and no invasion came. Adolf Hitler, the German Nazi dictator, believed that Britain would now give in without further fighting. When Britain surrendered, Hitler planned to reach an arrangement with the British. He would make a peace treaty – but of course it would contain very favourable terms for the conquering Germans. Hitler was very surprised when his offer was refused!

Now Hitler understood he could only achieve a British surrender by force. He began to assemble an invading army at channel ports in the Netherlands, Belgium and France – all countries that were occupied by his armies. But no invasion could take place until the Luftwaffe (the German air force) had defeated Britain's RAF (the Royal Air Force) in battle.

In theory, the Luftwaffe should have had no difficulty in doing that. The German air force had four times more aeroplanes than the RAF. The Luftwaffe was also conveniently based in airfields in France, Norway and Holland. It could easily fly over and attack southern England, and so wipe out Britain's air power.

Hitler's invasion of Britain, code-named "Operation Sealion", was planned for September. Admiral Raeder, the German navy's Commander-in-Chief, said that his forces would be ready by then. Marshal Hermann Goering, who was in charge of the Luftwaffe, began a heavy air offensive in July 1940. Goering believed that they would destroy the RAF in just four days.

The British government knew the RAF had to have many more fighter aircraft, and so the production of planes had to be quickly increased. Lord Beaverbrook was in charge of aircraft production under the newly appointed Prime Minister, Winston Churchill. Beaverbrook appealed to the public to give as much scrap metal as they could. The metal would speed up aircraft production, while more pilots were recruited and trained to fly them in battle.

Mountains of scrap metal – from saucepans to railings – were donated. The metal was recycled to build Hurricane and Spitfire fighter planes. Hundreds more pilots were trained. But Germany already had 2,600 fighter planes ready for action. Most of them were the new Messerschmitt Me109s, a highly efficient and well-designed plane. An air armada of heavy bombers and night fighters, including a wide range from the Dornier, Heinkel and Junkers factories, were ready to attack Britain.

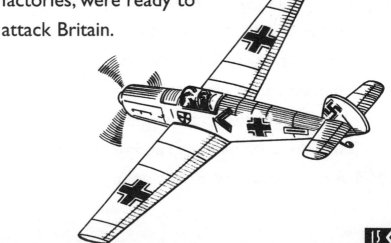

At this time the RAF had only Spitfires and Hurricanes, and a few old Bristol Blenheim bombers – no more than 700 operational aircraft in all. More planes were quickly produced and rolled out to airfields. More pilots came forward to fly the planes to defend Britain. Many Americans, Canadians, Australians and New Zealanders volunteered. So did many European pilots whose countries had been invaded by Germany, such as the Free French, and Czech, Belgian and Polish volunteers.

To lift the nation's morale and prepare
the British people for the coming battles,
Prime Minister Churchill delivered one of
his most famous rallying speeches. "Let us
brace ourselves to our duty, and so bear
ourselves that if the British Government
and Empire last a thousand years, men will
say: 'This was their finest hour.'"

Before starting the invasion, Hitler
decided to target the merchant navy ships
that brought food and fuel to Britain via the
Channel ports of Portsmouth and Dover.

These attacks became an introduction to the Battle of Britain. Britain and Germany both suffered heavy losses, but British pilots, radar operators and ground controllers learned a lot about fighting defensive air operations.

The air attacks on ships had met fierce British resistance, so Goering decided to begin the second phase of the air battle. Germany would bomb the airfields in the south of England, from which the RAF fighters and their pilots operated.

Goering code-named the date for this attack, 13 August 1940, as "Eagle Day". His plan was for an armada of German aircraft to attack Britain in force on that one day, overwhelming the RAF by sheer force of numbers. But the British radar system, although not the most advanced in the world, gave good warning of the approach of German aircraft. This meant that pilots and planes were able to get airborne quickly, and engage the German fighters in battle.

Douglas Turley-George, a Spitfire pilot, had vivid memories of this action:

> "The 109s (German Messerschmitt Me109 fighters) were coming at us from above as we struggled for height. I remember a 109 attacking me from the port side."

Turley-George tried to turn towards the enemy aircraft, hearing the loud bangs of cannon shells as they struck his Spitfire. "Even through the pounding fear I admired his marksmanship," he remembered of the German pilot. "A few seconds later, with my aeroplane miraculously still answering apparently normally to the controls, I dived out of the fire to return to base."

But Turley-George's plane was in much worse shape than he had imagined, and his engine cut out on the way back to the airfield. Desperately he searched for a safe place to land. Finally he found a farm field that looked flat enough, and crash-landed in the corn, ruining much of the crop. The farmer was furious! He demanded to know why Turley-George "couldn't have landed in the next field"!

Like the angry farmer, Sybil Eccles saw the Battle of Britain from a completely different viewpoint to that of a fighter pilot. In mid-August 1940, she wrote a letter to her husband, David, who was working at the British Embassy in Madrid. This letter vividly captures the atmosphere of the deadly duel in the sky above Britain.

"I was struggling with the young ones to get them ready for a walk. John sauntered in and said, 'They're having a practice, I suppose. I've just heard an air-raid warning.' But I always underestimated the astonishing accuracy of my eldest, and just pooh-poohed the poor boy, and went up the hill – and a good thing we did, for we had a fine sight of it all from the pub.

Halfway up, the boys ran off – a stream of aeroplanes came over at great speed and

presently columns of smoke
rose from Ludgershall... One
could see the salvoes hit the
ground in rapid succession
and the puffs go up. Presently
the Spitfires were overhead and
we watched a chase... Our
trio thoroughly enjoyed
themselves and made a
striking example of
the insensibility to
danger of the young."

In direct contrast, the
real danger of the
situation is more vividly
described in the story
of a pilot called
"Cocky" Dundas. His
account is of part of

Cocky Dundas's plane was the worst hit of all in that attack. Afterwards, he remembered that "white smoke filled the cockpit and I couldn't see the sky or the Channel coast 12,000 feet below. Centrifugal force pressed me against the side of the cockpit and I knew I was spinning. I felt panic and terror and I thought, 'this is the end!'"

Dundas knew that he had to get out of the aircraft fast. He pulled the handle where the canopy locked into the top of the windscreen. The canopy moved back an inch, then jammed again.

Then Dundas's Spitfire began to spiral downwards, spinning wildly while he pulled and wrenched and hammered at the hood to try to open it. But Dundas still couldn't get the canopy open wide enough to escape through the gap. He was cutting his hands and tearing his nails, tugging desperately. It was his only chance of survival. Suddenly the canopy opened, and he clambered out of the aircraft just in time.

Fortunately his parachute opened immediately, and Dundas floated safely in the breeze. He watched his plane hit the ground below him and then explode. A flock of sheep scattered outwards from the cloud of dust, smoke and flame the plane created as it crashed.

Cocky Dundas had splinters in his left leg and had dislocated his shoulder, but he knew he was lucky to be alive. For all the lucky escapes of pilots like him, Britain had lost more than 150 pilots by mid-August 1940. Only 99 men had been trained to replace them. Britain had also lost more than 180 fighter planes in the air, and 30 more had been destroyed on the ground. So far, only 170 aircraft had been built to replace those missing planes.

Flight Lieutenant Philip Cox, of 501 Squadron, was one of the brave pilots who was killed in action during the Battle of Britain. The following letter was written to his mother by his commanding officer.

Dear Mrs Cox

It is with great regret and very deep sympathy that I write.

Your son... was lost on July 27th. At the time he was killed he was leading the squadron in my absence. The squadron fought an engagement in the late afternoon off the south east coast. No one actually saw him go, but it was confirmed that he crashed into the sea... (He) was such a splendid fellow and most popular with everyone he met. He was always cheerful and possessed a charming manner.

He was a first class pilot and leader...

Yours sincerely

HAV Hogan

By September 1940 German tactics had changed, and London became the main target for the German bombers. Night after night the capital was attacked. While their homes were destroyed, most civilians sheltered in special air-raid shelters and Underground stations. Other cities also faced a similar pounding, as the Luftwaffe tried to break Britain's morale. But Britain still refused to give in.

The RAF fought back bravely and successfully. Even in the worst-hit areas ordinary people stayed calm, and helped each other. Every night, firefighters and medical workers dealt with scenes of unimaginable horror, as massive fires were put out and people were pulled from the wreckage of their homes.

The Battle of Britain lasted for just 12 fierce and exhausting weeks. In the end, the resistance mounted by Britain made the Nazis lose heart. The Germans lost 1,700 aircraft and 2,500 aircrew. The RAF lost 550 pilots and 900 other personnel.

By October, Hitler decided to postpone Operation Sealion. By January 1941 he gave orders that all preparations for the invasion should end. Hitler had decided to turn his attention to the invasion of Russia.

The pilots who flew – and died – with the RAF were Britain's first line of defence against a Nazi invasion in 1940.

As Winston Churchill rightly said:

"Never in the field of human conflict
was so much owed
by so many to so few."

THE ONE THAT GOT AWAY

GREAT BRITAIN

London

Croydon

FRANCE

Oberleutnant Franz Von Werra was a resourceful and imaginative Luftwaffe pilot, and the only German prisoner of war to return to Germany via Britain, Canada and the United States.

Von Werra was shot down over Kent, in England, in 1940. His squadron of Messerschmitt Me109s was escorting German bombers on a raid over Croydon, just south of London.

Franz Von Werra crash-landed his Messerschmitt in a field. He managed to get out of the wreckage with only a few bumps and bruises. But, almost immediately, he was taken prisoner near the site of his crash. Von Werra spent the night in a police cell. The next day he was taken under armed guard to an interrogation centre in Kensington Palace Gardens, in London.

Von Werra, like any captured service person, refused to give any information

except his name, rank and serial number. He was taken to another interrogation centre at Trent Park, in a suburb of north London. There Von Werra was questioned for two weeks, but he still refused to give more details. Eventually he was transferred to POW (Prisoner of War) Camp One, at Grizedale Hall in the Lake District. The camp was specially designed to hold captured officers. Most of Von Werra's companions were U-boat (German submarine) officers. The most senior officers formed a three-man council, which kept discipline among the prisoners, and liaised with their British captors to make sure everyone was properly treated.

Von Werra applied in secret to the council at Grizedale Hall for permission to make an escape bid. The council agreed.

On 7 October 1940, Von Werra joined a cross-country march, organized to give the German POWs some exercise. The march was closely supervised by British prison-camp guards. During a rest stop, however, Von Werra jumped over a stone wall and hid. The guards didn't see him go, but a couple of local women did. They frantically waved handkerchiefs at the guards, trying to direct their attention to Von Werra.

But the other German POWs were determined to help their fellow prisoner. They waved back enthusiastically to the women, and convinced the guards that the women were just being friendly! It was not until a head count was taken back at the camp that Von Werra's escape was discovered. With the other prisoners' help, he had gained a little time.

The local police and the Home Guard (the volunteer defence force) were both alerted. A large-scale hunt was mounted to find the missing man. Von Werra was found hiding in a stone hut by members of the Home Guard but somehow, in the rain and darkness, he managed to escape yet again!

The resourceful Von Werra kept his freedom for another five days. He stole food, and hid wherever he could. But a vigilant shepherd caught sight of him on 12 October 1940, and he was recaptured and returned to Grizedale Hall. There he was punished for his escape attempt with 21 days in solitary confinement.

But before he could complete the sentence, Von Werra was transferred to POW (Officers) Transit Camp No 13 near Swanwick in Derbyshire. Once there, he was determined to escape again. Von Werra formed a code-named "Swanwick Construction Company" with another prisoner. Their plan was named after the nearby village, but the activities of the "construction company" were not only secret, but also unusual ones for a construction company.

The Swanwick Construction Company's plan was to dig an escape tunnel. Von Werra

chose other prisoners to help with the
tunnelling. Digging the tunnel was easy,
because the prisoners had found some
shovel-like scoops used by the British to
remove burning incendiary bombs in the
event of an air raid. What was difficult,
however, was disposing of the soil dug out
of the tunnel. The earth underneath the
Garden House, where the German
prisoners were held, was heavy clay. If they
dumped it in the open, it would alert the
camp's guards.

At first the prisoners got rid of the earth by filling in the wall cavities and the spaces underneath floorboards. Then one prisoner discovered an empty water tank under a slab in the garden. That made a perfect container for the clay from the tunnel. Now the work could progress quickly. The prisoners even had a ventilation system, made out of tin cans, to get fresh air to the diggers.

Eventually, the five men who finished the tunnel won the right to use it. Their plan was to try to reach Ireland, which was a neutral country, not involved in the war. If they couldn't do that, they would try to stow away on any neutral ship leaving the English ports.

Von Werra decided not to stick with the other men. He thought their ideas were too limited. He spoke English well, and he chose to try out an outrageous idea. He would steal an aircraft from a Royal Air Force base, and fly himself back to Germany!

Von Werra decided to pretend to be a Dutch pilot from a RAF base at Dyce, near Aberdeen in Scotland. His story was to be that he – the "Dutch pilot" – had crash-landed north of Derby while on a secret test flight, and had been ordered to the nearest base to pick up another aircraft. Von Werra planned to turn up at an RAF base and steal an aircraft. He was confident he could get through security at the base, but he knew it would be more difficult to take the aircraft.

Von Werra worked on the idea until he had perfected it. He knew his lack of

identity papers wouldn't be a problem,
because no pilot would carry them on a
flying mission. But every pilot in the RAF
wore an identity disc at all times. He knew
he would have to produce one somehow.
Eventually, Von Werra managed to make a
forged disc. For the Dutch pilot's clothes,
he borrowed a flying suit from one of his
fellow prisoners, and flying boots
from another.

When the 16-metre tunnel was completed in a month, all five prisoners could hardly believe their good luck. They had dug quickly and efficiently, and they had not been discovered. Now all they had to do was to escape!

The breakout took place at night on 20 December 1940, and went according to plan. After that, though, things quickly started to go wrong. Two of the German prisoners waited in a bus queue, and then boarded the bus. They asked the conductor for tickets in good English, but they couldn't understand the question they were asked! The conductor had a strong Derbyshire accent, and wanted to know if the men wanted "single or return" – but the prisoners couldn't reply! Thinking quickly, they pretended to be drunk, hoping that would explain their strange behaviour.

It seemed to work, but the men feared they had aroused suspicion. They got off the bus and stole a bicycle – which belonged to the local policeman! The prisoners were arrested and taken to the police station. There one of them managed to escape again. He got as far as Sheffield before he was re-arrested.

The other two prisoners were also recaptured, just outside Manchester. They had hitched a lift in a lorry, but the driver had become suspicious, and had contacted the police.

Von Werra was better at deception than the other four, and his knowledge of English language and mannerisms was good. He persuaded a railway station clerk to telephone the nearest RAF base for him.

The clerk told the duty officer at the Hucknall RAF base Von Werra's story. The duty officer was not completely convinced by it, but he agreed to send a car to pick Von Werra up from the railway station.

Then, with his suspicions mounting, the duty officer at Hucknall tried to put through a call to the base at Dyce where Von Werra claimed to have come from. While he was waiting on the line, the duty officer – face to face with Von Werra – asked for identification. But when Von Werra reached for his identity disc, he found that his body heat had melted the forged disc. What was he going to do?

Luck came to Von Werra's aid, as it often did. While the duty officer was trying to talk to Dyce on a very bad line, Von Werra slipped out through a toilet window. On the airfield he found a brand-new Hawker Hurricane fighter being fitted out, and convinced the ground crew that he was a test pilot. He even took a parachute and signed out the aircraft! He was seated in the cockpit at the controls, ready to leave, when the duty officer caught up and arrested him.

Von Werra was returned to Camp 13
with the other recaptured prisoners. But
amazingly enough, another chance for him
to escape came when all the prisoners at
Camp 13 were shipped to Canada.

When the prisoners were on board the
Canadian Pacific's *Duchess of York*, a
special guard was put on Von Werra. The
ship sailed for Nova Scotia on 10 January
1941. During the voyage, Von Werra
suggested to the other POWs that they

should plan to take over the liner and sail
it to the nearest German-held port. But the
others saw too many problems with the
proposed mutiny, and the idea was
abandoned.

Once in Canada, and still under heavy
guard, the POWs were put on a train
heading for a new camp on the shore of
Lake Superior. Von Werra immediately began
to plan another escape. He thought his best
shot would be to cross the St Lawrence
River, which forms a natural border
between part of Canada and the United
States of America. (At that time, the USA
was still neutral, and hadn't yet joined the
Allies in the war against Hitler.)

Von Werra decided to jump from the
train taking them to the camp at Lake
Superior. Other prisoners helped him to

squeeze through a window. They also distracted the guards on the train, so that his disappearance wouldn't be noticed for some time.

Von Werra fell into a snowdrift beside the railway line, and wasn't hurt. He started to walk through the freezing Canadian winter weather to the St Lawrence River.

As resourceful as ever, he got a lift part of the way – and even managed to get a map of the area from a roadside garage.

Von Werra tried to walk across the frozen St Lawrence River to New York State, on the opposite bank of the river. The ice had melted on the American side, however, so he couldn't get all the way across on foot. Von Werra was undaunted. He returned to the Canadian side of the river, and stole a boat. Then he dragged the boat across the ice, and got into it and paddled to shore where the ice had melted. Finally, Von Werra had succeeded in reaching the USA, although his ears were badly frost-bitten.

After getting a lift to the nearest town, Von Werra was charged with entering the United States illegally. He could cope with that! He knew that when he convinced the authorities that he was really an escaped German POW, they would have to release him from prison.

Von Werra made headlines in America and Canada on 22 January 1941, and became a media hero. He was released from prison on a $5,000 bail bond, which was paid by the German consul. The consul also sent Von Werra a train ticket to New York, and looked after him at the German Consulate there.

Once he was in New York, Von Werra wrote a report on his interrogation in London and told the story of his amazing escape. But the American authorities decided to return him to Canada, so Von Werra needed to escape yet again. He fled to neutral Mexico on 24 March 1941, and made his way back to Germany through Rio de Janeiro, in Brazil.

Once he was back in Germany, Von Werra was awarded the Knights' Cross for his exploits. He wrote a book describing his life as a prisoner of war, and supplied the Luftwaffe with valuable information. He even began flying Messerschmitt Me109s again. But on 25 October 1941, Von Werra's plane had engine failure and crashed into the sea off the coast of the Netherlands. His body was never recovered, and neither was his plane.

That was his greatest disappearance – and his last.

SUICIDE PILOTS

At 6.50 a.m. on 14 May 1945, a radar plotter on board an American aircraft carrier in the Pacific Ocean reported an isolated "blip" at 2,500 metres, about 40 kilometres away.

The anti-aircraft guns of the enormous ship were immediately swivelled to point in that direction, ready to fire. At 6.54 a.m. the aircraft came into sight. It was Japanese.

The plane flew straight towards the carrier, but then it suddenly changed course and disappeared into the clouds again. Three minutes later the aircraft appeared again, losing altitude. What was going on?

The anti-aircraft guns on the ship began to fire at the plane, and it returned into the cloud cover. The aircraft carrier's guns continued to fire, but the crew were not yet very worried. All the ship's aircraft were either in the air, or de-fuelled and parked below decks. What harm could one small plane do to the massive carrier?

Suddenly the plane came out of the clouds again, and began a sharp dive towards the carrier at high speed. The horrified men on the ship watching the plane coming towards them didn't know it was flown by a "kamikaze" pilot — but they were soon to understand what that meant.

In Japanese tradition, honour is supremely important and life is relatively unimportant. There has been no clearer example of this than the suicide – or kamikaze – pilots. Their actions are like those of modern suicide terrorist bombers.

A *kami kaze* in Japanese folklore means a "divine wind". In one story, the divine wind was sent by the sun goddess to destroy the ships of the Mongol ruler Kublai Khan, whose armies threatened Japan in the thirteenth century.

Nearly seven centuries later, the Japanese people were searching for another kind of divine wind to defeat the Allied fleet. The Allies were winning the war in the Pacific, and would soon demand Japan's surrender. That defeat would mean the loss of Japan's honour.

In October 1944, Vice-Admiral Takijiro Onishi, the Commander of the Japanese First Air Fleet, made a speech to twenty-six potential kamikaze fighter pilots. This is what he said.

"My sons, who can raise our country from the desperate situation in which she finds herself. Japan is in grave danger. The salvation of our country is now beyond the power of the Minister of State, the General Staff and lowly commanders like myself.

It can only come from spirited young men such as you. Thus on behalf of your hundred million countrymen, I ask you for this sacrifice and pray for your success. You are already gods, without earthly desires. But one thing you want to know is that your crash dive is not in vain. Regrettably, we will not be able to tell you the results. But I shall watch your efforts to the end and report your deeds to the Throne. You may all rest assured on that point. I ask you to do your best."

The mention of the throne referred to the Japanese emperor. The young men were being asked to give their lives to serve him, and many were inspired to do so. Pilot Isao Matsuo of the 701 Air Group was one kamikaze volunteer. On 28 October 1944, he wrote this letter to his parents:

Beloved parents

Please congratulate me. I have been given a splendid opportunity to die. This is my last day. The destiny of our homeland hinges on the decisive battle in the Southern Seas, where I shall fall like a blossom from a radiant cherry tree. I shall be a shield for [the ship] Tenno and die cleanly along with my squadron leader and other friends. I wish that I could be born seven times, each time to smite the enemy. [Japanese classics teach that there are Seven Evils which will attack Japan.] How I appreciate this chance to die like a man. I am grateful from the depths of my heart to the parents who have reared me with their constant prayers and tender love. And I am grateful as well to my squadron leader and superior officers who have looked after me as if I were their own son and given me such careful training.

Thank you, my parents, for the twenty-three years during which you have cared for me and inspired me. I hope that my present deed will in some small way repay what you have done for me. Think well of me and know that your Isao died for our country. This is my last wish, and there is nothing else that I desire. Please take good care of yourselves. How glorious is the Giretsu Tai (Special Heroic Task Force Unit) whose bombers will attack the enemy. Our goal is to dive against the aircraft carriers of the enemy. Movie cameramen have been here to take our pictures. It is possible that you may see us in newsreels at the theatre. We are sixteen warriors manning the bombers. May our death be as sudden and clean as the shattering of crystal.

Written at Manila on the eve of our sortie.

Isao

To those who watched from the USS *Enterprise*, the Japanese kamikaze pilot seemed to have no doubt about what he was going to do. He was going to crash his plane on to the 17,000-tonne aircraft carrier! By now all the ship's anti-aircraft guns were firing at the plane, which had been hit. It was trailing flame and smoke, but the Japanese aircraft was still heading directly for the ship.

Sailors on the *Enterprise* threw themselves flat on their faces. The aircraft crashed on to the flight deck with an enormous impact, shaking the entire vessel. About 40 metres of the flight deck was badly damaged, and part of the lift used to raise aircraft from the hangars was thrown more than 100 metres in the air.

The explosion killed 14 crew members. Some of the shaken survivors marched past the corpse of the pilot, which lay on the deck of the carrier next to his mangled plane. The survivors gazed in horrified fascination at the body. Many of them noticed that the buttons of his tunic were stamped in relief with an unusual pattern – a cherry blossom with three petals. That pattern was, in fact, the insignia of the Kamikaze Corps.

Isao would have felt that his was a hero's death. He would have hoped that the manner of his death had a kind of elegance and grace. A kamikaze pilot had a particular identity, and always dressed stylishly, sporting a loosely knotted white scarf around his neck. Under his leather flying helmet he wore the *hachimaki*, a replica of the headband worn by medieval Japanese Samurai warriors. He also wore a *sennin-bari*, a cloth or silk band stitched with red, around his waist. This was meant to have a mystical power, and to symbolize a bulletproof vest.

Many kamikaze pilots also carried a personal patriotic flag. Usually this took the form of a square of white cloth with a *hinomaru* on it (the Japanese emblem of a round sun). The sun was surrounded by words praising the spirit of suicide.

The pilots and their proud families received the title of "Very Honourable". All kamikaze pilots were given special privileges like extra food rations and privileged seats at ceremonies. They had their pictures in the newspapers. The same applied to their families. Even Japanese news reports on the radio were often read out over the background music of the kamikaze pilots singing the Samurai song:

*In serving on the seas, be a corpse
saturated with water.*

*In serving on the land, be a corpse covered
with weeds.*

*In serving in the sky, be a corpse that
challenges the clouds.*

*Let us all die close by the side of the
Emperor.*

The Japanese were very proud of their kamikaze pilots.

There was some Allied respect for the suicide pilots, too. One of the American naval officers at the Battle of Okinawa in the Pacific War remembered it like this.

"Few missiles or weapons have ever spread such terror, such scorching burns, such searing death, as did the kamikaze in his self-destroying onslaughts on our ships.

And naval history has few parallels to the sustained courage, resourcefulness and fighting spirit that the crews of these vessels displayed day after day in the Battle for Okinawa."

But it must have been very difficult for the Japanese men who didn't want to die in this way. This memory from a young trainee is particularly vivid:

"After a long time, he [the commander] spoke sonorously: 'Any of you unwilling to give your lives as divine sons of the great Nippon Empire will not be required to do so. Those incapable of accepting this honour will raise their hands. Now!'

Hesitantly, timidly, one hand goes up and then another and another – six in all. I can choose to live or die. But somehow… of course I want to live. My hands remain at my sides, trembling. I want to raise them, but I can't. Am I a coward? I can't do it.

Captain Tsuba fixes those who have responded in his stare. 'It is good to know exactly where we stand.' They are summoned before him. 'Here, gentlemen,' he points to the ashen faces, 'are six men who have openly admitted to their disloyalty. Since they are completely devoid of honour, it is our duty to provide them with some. These men shall be in the first attack group!'

The breath, held so long within me, struggled out. I want to draw in more air, to expel it with relief, but something clenches inside. Six men from my squadron have just been picked for death."

This account supports the theory that the choice to be a kamikaze pilot was not always voluntary. The reality was that some kamikaze had to be drugged and forcibly strapped into their cockpits. Another method used to make pilots volunteer to be kamikaze was to blackmail them, threatening that their families would be severely punished unless the pilots agreed to commit suicide.

But, as Isao Matsuo's account shows, there is also evidence that many of the suicide pilots genuinely felt that their sacrifice was in defence of their homeland. The sacrifice was also made for their way of life, and the Japanese imperial family. To the pilots that was the heart of their country and its glorious past.

The following poem was found on the body of a kamikaze pilot:

Not the sea
Yet to the very bottom of those brimming
  waters
The moon will illuminate a blameless heart.

He was truly part of the "divine wind"
that blew against the enemies of Japan.

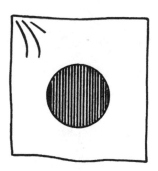

HIROSHIMA

Dr Michihiko Hachiya was at home in Hiroshima on 6 August 1945, when the first atomic bomb, code-named "Little Boy", was dropped by an American Boeing B-29 Superfortress bomber. Dr Hachiya remembered the beauty of the early morning, before the terrible impact of the bomb on the unsuspecting city.

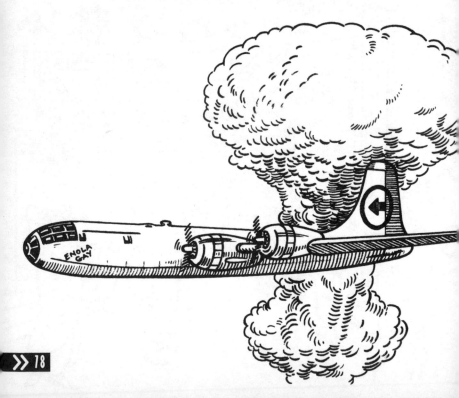

"The hour was early, the morning still, warm and beautiful. Shimmering leaves reflected the sunlight from a cloudless sky as I gazed absently through wide-flung doors opening to the south. Clad in vest and pants I lay on the living room floor exhausted because I had just spent a sleepless night on duty as a air-raid warden in my hospital."

Hiroshima Diary, Dr Michihiko Hachiya

Dr Hachiya was startled by a strong flash of light, and then another. He saw a stone lantern in his garden suddenly become brilliantly lit, and he wondered whether this strange occurrence was caused by sparks from a passing tram, or a magnesium flare.

Still numb and bewildered, Dr Hachiya found himself unable to understand what was happening. First the bright, sunny early morning world disappeared into a totally dismal, dark haze. Then he noticed that a wooden column that held up one of the walls of his house now leaned at an angle. The roof was no longer supported.

Dr Hachiya instinctively knew that he had to get outside as fast as he could, but he still felt a dream-like lack of reality. Nevertheless, he found himself moving through the rubble that had once been his home and out into his garden. Suddenly a tremendous weakness overcame him and he stumbled to a halt.

It felt to Dr Hachiya as if the world had ended. When he glanced up at the darkness of the sky, he realised that something unknown and terrible had happened. Then he began to feel pain stirring in him, and becoming increasingly intense. The right side of his body was cut and bleeding.

He recalled: "A large splinter was protruding from a wound in my thigh and something warm trickled into my mouth… Embedded in my neck was a sizeable fragment of glass which I matter-of-factly dislodged, and with the detachment of one stunned and shocked, I studied it and my bloodstained hand."

Dr Hachiya survived the dropping of the bomb on Hiroshima, but thousands of others didn't. Many people around the world thought the bombing of civilians with such a devastating weapon was indefensible.

Tsutomu Yamaguchi's eyewitness account is still more startling – and shocking – than Dr Hachiya's. In 1945, he was a worker in the Mitsubishi shipbuilding company in Hiroshima. He was on his way to work when the bomb was dropped more than a mile away. "Suddenly there was a flash like the lighting of a huge magnesium flare. As I prostrated myself there came a terrific explosion. I was lifted two feet from the ground."

Mr Yamaguchi lay in the road, dazed, for some time. When he opened his eyes he could see nothing but darkness. Eventually

his eyes adjusted and he could see that he
was covered by a cloud of dust, so thick
that it was black. He saw what seemed to
be thousands of flickering lamps all over the
streets and in the fields. Then he realised
the lights were little circles of flame, each
about the size of a doughnut. Hundreds of
them were hanging on the leaves of the
potato plants in a nearby field.

Mr Yamaguchi looked towards the city
of Hiroshima and saw a huge, mushroom-
shaped cloud rising high up into the sky.
"It was an immense, evil-looking pillar. It
seemed to be reflecting every shade in the
spectrum, turning first one colour and then
another."

Mr Yamaguchi had deep burns on his face
and arms. He didn't know what to do, but
stumbled into the potato field to try and

escape somehow from the cloud. He headed for a big tree, but found himself crawling from bush to bush instead, getting incredibly thirsty as he crawled.

Mr Yamaguchi saw a group of teenage boys stripped of their clothes by the blast, except for their torn underpants. As the boys came nearer to him, he saw that blood was streaming down their bodies from fierce cuts, and their flesh was burnt a deep red. At first it also seemed to him that their burnt bodies were growing green grass — which was a macabre sight. Then Mr Yamaguchi realised that hundreds of blades of grass had been driven deep into their flesh by the force of the blast.

Mr Yamaguchi wondered what the effect of the explosion would be on him. Its effect on the boys was all too obvious.

After reading these eyewitness accounts, it might be difficult to understand why the Allies used such a weapon against the Japanese people. But the Allies were desperate to end the war.

The Germans had finally surrendered to the Allies in May 1945. That brought the war in Europe to an end. But Japan was still fighting against the Allied forces in Asia and the Pacific. Most of Japan's shipping had been sunk or badly damaged, and the air force crippled. Japan's factories had been bombed, and its food supplies were shrinking. But still the Japanese government refused to surrender.

For the Japanese, unconditional surrender

was unthinkable. That would have been a violation of everything they believed in. No Japanese minister was prepared to give the order to stop fighting.

The Allies tried to decide what to do about this problem. After the Potsdam Conference in July 1945, the American President (Harry Truman), the British Prime Minister (Winston Churchill) and the Russian leader (Joseph Stalin) decided to present Japan with an ultimatum. They offered unconditional surrender, or destruction. Those choices were immediately rejected by Japan.

Truman and Churchill decided the bomb would be dropped on Hiroshima on 6 August 1945. Even then the Japanese didn't surrender, and so a second bomb was dropped on Nagasaki three days later.

Just 13 days after the bomb had been dropped on Hiroshima, the death toll in that region of Japan had risen to nearly 100,000 people. In the years that followed, the death toll continued to rise further because of nuclear fallout from the bomb. Radioactive dust penetrated the nervous system and tissues of the citizens of Hiroshima. That caused a wide range of fatal illnesses and deformities. Animals and plants were also affected.

Churchill attempted to justify the British and American decision to drop a nuclear bomb. This is what he said:

"To avert a vast, indefinite butchery, to bring the war to an end, to give peace to the world, to lay healing hands upon its tortured people by a manifestation of overwhelming power at the cost of a few explosives seemed, after all our toils and perils, a miracle of development. British consent to the use of the weapon had been given on 4th July 1945. The final decision now lay in the main with President Truman, who had the weapon. But I never doubted what it would be, nor have I ever doubted since that he was right."

In his memoirs, Truman wrote this: "Let there be no mistake about it. I regarded the bomb as a military weapon and never had any doubt it should be used."

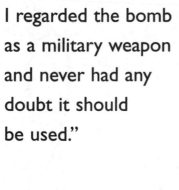

Many historians now believe that the atom bomb was not needed to force Japan's surrender. Even at the time there were influential people who opposed the decision to drop it.

Admiral Leaky, who was Chief of Staff in turn to two presidents, Roosevelt and Truman, was outspoken on the subject.

"I was not taught to make war in that fashion, and wars cannot be won by destroying women and children."

Admiral King, the US naval Commander-in-Chief, stated that the naval blockade alone would have starved the Japanese into submission, "had we been willing to wait".

The result of the decision to use atom bombs changed the world for ever. It was not just a disaster for Japanese people. It also unleashed the threat of nuclear war – and that is a threat that still looms over the world today.

But the bombing of Hiroshima and Nagasaki certainly did end the war.

On 2 September 1945, members of the Japanese government signed what was called an 'instrument of surrender'. It was signed on board the battleship USS *Missouri*, in Tokyo Bay. In fact, this was no more than a formal ceremony. The real defeat of Japan happened on 14 August 1945, when the Emperor announced his country's surrender on terms laid down by the Allies.

With that ceremony, the Second World War finally ended, six years and a day after the conflict had begun with Hitler's attack on Poland.

GLOSSARY

Allies
   Countries such as Britain, France and the USA that
   fought together against Germany, Japan, Italy and some
   other countries during World War Two.

Aircraft carrier
   A large ship with an immense top deck, on which
   aircraft can take off and land.

Atomic bomb
   A weapon of mass destruction. Its immense power
   comes from the conversion of uranium atoms into
   energy.

Dictator
   A leader who imposes his will on a country using
   military force and intimidation instead of elections.

Free French
   The French fighters who fought with the Allies after
   France had surrendered to the Germans.

Home Guard
   A volunteer unit formed to defend the homeland
   while the regular army is fighting somewhere else.

Kamikaze
A Japanese suicide bomber whose job it was to crash his bomb-laden aircraft into enemy targets. The word comes from the Japanese kami kaze or "divine wind".

Luftwaffe
The German word for 'air force'.

Nazi
A member of Adolf Hitler's National Socialist Party and supporter of its policies.

POW
Short for "prisoner of war". A member of a country's armed forces captured by the enemy in battle.

U-boat
U-boat is a translation from the German of U-boot. It is short for Unterseeboot or an undersea boat.

WAR AT SEA

The enemy was all around. The Luftwaffe (the German air force), the U-boats and the warships of the German navy all lay in wait. And there were always the icebergs, and the freezing fog, of the Barents Sea.

WAR ON LAND

The first wave of troops was mostly killed, cut down as they came ashore. Then the second wave of troops had to advance over the bodies of the dead. Survival was their main instinct.

WAR AT HOME

The boys had a meeting and decided to take as many knives and forks as they could get their hands on in order to defend themselves. But they realised that knives and forks would be little use against the Nazis' guns.

WAR IN THE AIR

Dundas's Spitfire began to spiral downwards, spinning wildly while he pulled and wrenched and hammered at the hood to open it. But Dundas still couldn't get the canopy open wide enough to escape through the gap.